All right reserved. No part of this publication may be reproduced, distributed or transmitted in any form or by any means, including photocopying, recording, other electronic or mechanical methods without prior written permission of the publisher except in case of brief quotation embodied in critical reviews and certain noncommercial use permitted by copyright law.

Contents

What Is Concierge Service? Meaning & Business Models 3

The Concierge Services Business Model 5

The Future of Concierge Services 10

What is a luxury concierge? 17

Why do you Need a High-End Concierge? 19

How to select the best luxury concierge for you? 20

Best Luxury Concierge Services in the World 23

The Surprising Truth Behind Starting a Personal Concierge Business 35

Guide to Starting a Concierge Service Business and Attracting Clients 44

Top Concierge Skills 48

How to Start a Personal Concierge Business 54

What Is a Personal Concierge Business? 55

How Much Money Can You Make as a Personal Concierge? 57

How Much does it Cost to Become a Personal Concierge? 59

How to Get Your First Client 63

Additional Tips to Make More Money as a Personal Concierge 65

Steps to Naming your Concierge Business 69

More Tips for naming your concierge business 76

Introduction

Do you ever wake up and feel like there should be someone to do your errands while you sit back and relax? To plan your entire holiday or a date, instead of you sitting in front of the computer screen for hours? Do you want an expert to be your personal assistant or your lifestyle manager?

Well, there are companies which provide such services. Their employees will do anything for you as long as it's legal, moral and ethical.

What is a Concierge?

Some say that the word 'concierge' is derived from a Latin word 'conservus' which translates to 'fellow slave', while some say that it has evolved from the French 'comte des cierges', which means 'the keeper of the candles', which was essentially the main duty of concierges during the Middle Ages. Nonetheless, the meaning and the duties of the concierges have changed over time. They now perform almost every task for top-level managers, VIP customers of banks and hotels, superstars, or anyone who have enough money to outsource their work to them.

So, what is a concierge?

A concierge is an individual or a company which is specialised in personal assistance or any other assistance services like household management, lifestyle management, transportation, travel and vacation planning, etc. and provides such personalized services to its clients (usually high-net-worth clients) at a variable price.

The idea is to save the time of the client by performing their routine or specialized tasks.

The Concierge Services Business Model

Concierge services are a fairly recent addition to the luxury industry; all thanks to the constantly changing business environment, the technological advancement, and the long working hours of the working professionals. Such limitations have resulted in lack of time in the life of the people. They now wish for either more time or someone who can do the work for them while they free their time for the things that matter. Concierge services business model capitalizes on this need.

Earlier, concierges used to be restricted to hotels or luxury apartment buildings and used to assist guests by making restaurant reservations, arranging spa service, recommending places to visit, booking transportation, etc. But now these individuals and companies have moved ahead and have specialized in a lot of tasks ranging from lining up tickets for concerts or special events, planning a holiday trip, doing the shopping errands, restaurant recommendation and reservations, etc.

The business models of different concierge services providers differ in the types of service provided and to whom it is provided. Some concierges help employers maintain good employer-employee relations, some deal in handling customer grievances, some concierges provide personal travel planning service, while some provide all these services by acting as a personal assistant or lifestyle managers.

Here are few concierge services business models that are prevalent today:

Concierge Medicine

Concierge medicine (also called boutique medicine, retainer-fee practice, direct care, and membership medicine) is a prevalent concept where the customer pays a flat/annual fee or a retainer in exchange of enhanced personalized care and better access to their doctors.

The concept was started in 1996 when a doctor from Seattle decided to ask his patients to pay an annual fee or a retainer in exchange for highly attentive medicine. The practice became famous in a short while and was accepted by a lot of doctors from all over the world.

The concierge medicine business model is a win-win model for both the doctors and the patients as the doctor doesn't have to manage a huge number of patients to make his ends meet and the patients get timely and personalized care and treatment from their doctor.

The retainer fee of such service range from few hundred dollars to tens of thousands of dollars per year. This may or may not be in addition to other charges and may or may not be covered by health insurance policies.

Lifestyle Management / Personal Concierge

Lifestyle management is a specialized service where the client outsources his personal tasks like daily errands management, pet sitting, house sitting, reservations, special events management, shopping etc. to a commercial firm or a professional.

These concierge brands use their expertise to save the time and provide exceptionally personalized luxurious service to their high-net-worthed clients.

Hotel Concierge

The hotel concierge is one of the oldest and most prevalent concierge services provided to VIP and high-net-worth clients. These concierges provide services like making recommending and making restaurant reservations, arranging spa services, booking transportation, procuring tickets for special events, attending and assisting client's guests etc.

Travel Concierge

The increasing popularity and affordability of travelling around the world have led to an addition of a new business model in the concierge industry: the travel concierge (or the trip concierge). The firms providing such services excel in travel planning and stand out by providing real-time information and 24×7 VIP support to their clients.

These companies know everything about the legal, social and cultural aspects of travelling in other countries and reserve/book everything beforehand for a seamless travel experience.

The Future of Concierge Services

Mobile devices and internet have changed the way concierges work. Today, a person residing in New York can ask his personal assistant residing in India to plan his trip to Egypt. All this can be done seamlessly with just one text message.

The industry is also not untapped and or under-marketed anymore. The developed technology has included AI to concierges, which has led to this industry opening gates to medium-level income clients.

Google assistant has all the plans to become your personal concierge. Assist is a famous automated assistant for messaging and voice. Haptik is building conversational AI for the world. Even Amazon has capitalized on this new trend with the introduction of Alexa.

With the new rise in the demand and supply of concierge service, the future of concierge services looks to be very good.

Go On, Tell Us What You Think!

Did we miss something? Come on! Tell us what you think of our article on Concierge services business model in the comments section.

A concierge service arranges any aspect of your life that you want, so you can maximise your free time. This ranges from planning holidays and booking restaurants, to helping run your everyday life (finding a good cleaner, the best gym, a gift for a loved one, etc).

Some will always prefer to do these things off their own back, but people are increasingly turning to concierge services to manage it for them.

We asked Emyr Thomas from concierge service Bon Vivant to tell us exactly why their members love them, and why you should have a concierge service on your speed dial too.

1. A Personal Pro-Active Service Tailored to You

2. Your Personal Guidebook and Search Engine

3. Save Time

4. Access an Expert's Insider Knowledge and Skills

5. The Convenience

6. Special Privileges and Complimentary Benefits

7. Know About the Latest 'Scene'

8. Grant you Exclusive Access

1. A Personal Pro-Active Service Tailored To You

The best concierge services will give you your own personal concierge, so that you deal with the same person at all times, for all requests. By learning your tastes and needs, this becomes a pro-active service, pre-empting what you would like to do.

2. **Your Personal Guidebook And Search Engine**

Researching holiday destinations, booking hotels and restaurants or sourcing a unique gift can sometimes be an arduous task. Why search blindly on the internet when you can ask for a personal recommendation from an expert with a huge book of contacts? This removes the unknown element, and puts you in trusted hands.

3. **Save Time**

Most clients will say that the main reason they use a concierge service is to free up precious time, enabling them to experience the things they love instead of spending time researching and booking them. A concierge service offers today's most priceless commodity – your time.

4. **Access An Expert's Insider Knowledge And Skills**

A good concierge service will always be looking for the best of everything to recommend to their clients, so you will have access to their insider knowledge and expertise. Want to know the best hotel in Paris? The best new restaurant in New York? The secluded beach resort in the Caribbean? The hidden bar in London? Your concierge will know.

5. **The Convenience**

It's not always about saving time or offering solutions to a problem you can't solve yourself – it's the convenience of having someone on hand, at the end of the phone or email, to help run your life, enabling you to maximise your free time.

6. Special Privileges And Complimentary Benefits

A true concierge service will strive to negotiate for special privileges and benefits for its members wherever possible. Upgrades at top luxury and boutique hotels, priority reservation and complimentary drinks at the best restaurants, free entry to exclusive clubs, or discounts at a host of other lifestyle services – a concierge service can add value, make you a VIP and save you money.

7. Know About The Latest 'Scene'

At Bon Vivant, through our member newsletters and blog, we keep our members informed of the best new hotels, new restaurant and bar openings, and the under-the-radar exclusives, so they can remain on the pulse wherever they are. We also get invited to new openings, launches and exclusive events; which we can pass onto our members.

8. Grant You Exclusive Access

A concierge service can obtain tickets to a variety of exclusive and sold out events. Music concerts, theatre and opera, sports games, premières, charity balls and events in the world of film, fashion and TV. VIP and hospitality access to seats and boxes at the O2

Arena, Wembley Arena and all other major venues is suddenly reachable.

What is a luxury concierge?

A concierge is a person or a company that is available to help you in your day-to-day life. Their services can range from planning and booking your family holidays to making restaurant reservations or getting you access to special events. Some concierge companies also provide financial services. Others might focus on event organisation or high-end travel reservations.

The word concierge probably comes from the old French word "comte des cierges." The comte des cierges was a servant responsible for maintaining the lighting and cleanliness of medieval palaces.

Today's concierge services extend far beyond just maintaining your candles lit. Concierges are highly skilled people who can add real value to your life by taking care of some essential and time-consuming tasks for you. They also have an extensive network to help you get VIP access to some of the most ultra-exclusive events and experiences around the world.

In general, you'll find two categories of concierge services today:

- **Personal concierge services**: if you want to hire the services of a concierge for yourself.
- **Corporate concierge services**: if a company wants to provide concierge services to its employees as an extra benefit.
- Some concierge companies specialise in real estate to give you access to unlisted properties.

Why do you Need a High-End Concierge?

Not everyone needs a luxury concierge. Some people like to manage every aspect of their life themselves. But if you're too busy and want to outsource some tasks, a personal concierge makes a lot of sense.

There are three main reasons for wealthy people to subscribe to a luxury concierge service:

- To save time;

- To get exclusive access to private events thanks to the concierge's network;
- To outsource time-consuming and repetitive tasks.

How to select the best luxury concierge for you?

There are more concierge services available to you today than ever before. While the range of options is great, it can be hard to compare services and understand where their expertise truly lies. Here are three tips to help you select the best luxury concierge for you.

Know what you want your concierge to do

Before comparing concierge companies, you first need to think carefully about what it is you want them to do for you. Are you looking for a general lifestyle concierge? Or a company that specialises in organising travel or dining experiences?

You'll see in our list below that certain concierge companies specialise in specific areas. This gives them a greater depth of expertise. But you might feel constraint after a while if you want your concierge to take on more responsibilities.

Choose the level of support that you want

Some concierge companies are now offering the option to choose between membership packages and on-demand services.

Membership packages are the traditional form of concierge support. You pay a monthly or yearly fee to be part of the concierge programme. In exchange, you get 24/7 support from your concierge who will, over time, get to know you and anticipate your needs.

On-demand concierge services are a new kind of experiences where you pay as you go. It's more transactional and focused on getting particular tasks done on a more ad-hoc basis.

Think about the geographic location of your concierge

Even though most concierge companies provide dedicated service around the clock, their expertise and network might not be relevant if you're travelling across the world.

Consider your lifestyle and decide if you prefer a concierge with experience in a particular state or country, or if you require the service of a global concierge company with a network of personnel across the world instead.

Best Luxury Concierge Services in the World

1. Quintessentially

Founded in 2000 by Ben Elliot, Paul Drummond and Aaron Simpson, Quintessentially is one of the best-known luxury concierge companies in the world. With over 60 offices across the world and a team of more than 1,500 concierge specialists,

Quintessentially is a leader in global luxury lifestyle services.

With an average client net worth of $36 million, Quintessentially concierges have fulfilled some extravagant requests over the years. They've been able, for example, to close the Sydney Harbour Bridge for a wedding proposal or to arrange a private dinner on an iceberg.

Coverage: Global

Services: Art, education, real estate, travel, personal shopping, private parties and celebrations, weddings and wine.

Website: www.quintessentially.com

2. Innerplace Concierge

Founded in 2002 in London, Innerplace Concierge is one of the world's most established luxury lifestyle concierges. With a restless demand for the exceptional, this award-winning members-only luxury concierge company offers crème de la crème access to the more glamorous side of life, with a bespoke, highly personal approach to your every wish and whim.

The concierge company specialises in securing access for its members to private members clubs, the finest restaurants, and select VIP events. They also have expertise in everything from bespoke luxury travel to art and even business connections.

Innerplace Concierge focuses on London where their influence is at its peak. Still, their unrivalled insider knowledge and exclusive, international connections allow them to cater to members worldwide.

With two unique tiers of membership, Innerplace Concierge caters to a select few UHNW individuals and families with their Red Membership and young, affluent professionals with their Lifestyle Membership.

Remarkably, they also offer a short term Jetset Membership for visitors travelling to London and a Corporate Membership option.

Coverage: Global (with a particular focus on the UK)

Services: Private members clubs, Restaurants, VIP events & tickets, Travel (Hotels, Villas, Jets, Experiences), Private parties & celebrations, Meet and Greets, Art, Business introductions

Website: www.innerplace.co.uk

3. John Paul Group

Founded in 2008 by David Amsellem, the John Paul Group is one of the leaders in global corporate concierge services. The group helps companies provide exceptional services to both clients and employees through loyalty programmes.

Accor Hotels acquired John Paul Group in 2016 and now counts over 1,000 concierges across 12 separate offices. Noteworthy request that they've been able to accomplish: renting a private Caribbean island for a "Robinson Crusoe"-themed trip.

Coverage: Global

Services: Travel, dining, ticketing, shopping, wellbeing, daily errands, childcare, automobile, events, real-estate, rare items, unique experiences.

Website: www.johnpaul.com

4. One Concierge

One Concierge is the first luxury concierge company to offer both membership and on-demand concierge services to its high-net-worth clients. With access to over 10,000 global service providers, One Concierge has one of the most comprehensive and exhaustive partnership programmes in the industry. Each partner is handpicked and screened by their specialists to ensure that they meet the most demanding expectations.

One Concierge handles concierge requests in more than 115 countries around the world.

Coverage: Global

Services: corporate, bespoke event organisation, lifestyle, private aviation.

Website: www.oneconcierge.com

5. **Knightsbridge Circle**

Founded by three former American Express Black Card employees, Knightsbridge Circle is an invitation-only very high-end private concierge service for the UHNWs. With client base with an average net worth of $800 million and a membership fee starting from $25,000, Knightsbridge Circle helps busy individuals save time and get exclusive invitations.

The group helped organise a wedding vow renewal with the Pope and a private dinner in front of The Last Supper of Leonardo da Vinci.

Coverage: Global

Services: travel, dining, private jet, event access, automobile, yachts, education, wealth management, bespoke event organisation, real estate, wellness.

Website: www.knightsbridgecircle.co.uk

6. Pure Entertainment Group

You might have seen some of the Pure Entertainment Group's work featured on the New York Times, Forbes, Elite Traveler Magazine or Robb Report. Pure Entertainment Group is a global bespoke event management and luxury concierge company that was founded in 2007.

The company offers high quality, highly tailored luxury concierge services to discerning high-net-worth and ultra-high-net-worth individuals and corporations around the world.

Coverage: Global

Services: dining, travel, unique experiences, VIP access, bespoke event organisation, shopping, transport, real estate.

Website: purentonline.com

7. The Fixer Lifestyle group

The Fixer Lifestyle group has over 12 years of experience managing UHNWIs and HNWIs demands. Based in the UK, the group specialises in providing luxury concierge services such as high-end restaurant reservations and access to VIP events. One of their most common requests from clients is to get access to sold-out shows such as the Paris Fashion Week, the Wimbledon final or Premier League matches.

Coverage: United Kingdom, Central Europe, UAE and North America

Services: home organising, lifestyle services, reservations, ticketing and travel.

Website: www.the-fixer.co.uk

8. Velocity Black

Velocity Black is one of the most progressive luxury concierges on our list. They combine deep human expertise with artificial intelligence to act as a lifestyle assistant that lives on your phone. Members get access to complimentary upgrades and preferred rates to major events, all at the press of a button.

Velocity Black was founded in the United Kingdom by ex- Goldman Sachs Zia Yusuf and Alex Macdonald with a team of ex-Amazon and ex-Uber executives. The concierge company has already delivered over 50 thousand experiences across more than 60 countries.

Coverage: Global

Services: travel, dining, event access, wellness.

Website: velocity.black

9. Nota Bene

Nota Bene started as a lifestyle magazine before evolving into a premium concierge company. Founded by Anthony Lassman, Nota Bene caters to discerning travellers seeking the most exclusive experiences. The team focuses on curating unique luxury travel experiences.

Coverage: Global

Services: travel and real estate.

Website: www.notabeneglobal.com

10. Bon Vivant

Founded by travel aficionados Emyr Thomas, Bon Vivant is one of London's leading concierge and lifestyle management service with global coverage. Their expertise naturally lies in luxury travel planning but also high-end restaurant reservations and access to exclusive and sold out events.

Coverage: Global

Services: travel, dining, VIP access and ticketing.

Website: bonvivant.co.uk

11. The Billionaire Concierge

The Billionaire Concierge is an invitation-only high-end luxury concierge service with offices mostly in the Dubai, Hong Kong, London, Los Angeles, Monaco, Moscow and Qatar. The company provides luxury lifestyle services to its HNW members, including shopping for rare watches and jewellery and celebrity chef private reservations.

The Surprising Truth Behind Starting a Personal Concierge Business

Last Updated NOVEMBER 13, 2020. Disclosure: We may receive compensation if you sign up for or purchase products linked below. Details on offers may change, and you should confirm them with the company prior to taking action.

Stephanie L. Howitt, Founder of SLH Lifestyle + Concierge, has stopped by today to help us navigate how to start a personal concierge service business.Back when I first started my home business, I longed to be a personal concierge. Running errands, keeping people organized and efficient – sounded like a great gig. But, I was living in a very rural area. There wasn't much need, and the travel costs involved wouldn't make it very profitable or affordable.

But, for some lucky gal or guy out there, it's perfect. And the target market is no longer just busy professionals it also now includes overstretched parents and the elderly.

Stephanie L. Howitt, Founder of SLH Lifestyle + Concierge, has stopped by to help us navigate how to start a personal concierge service business. You may be surprised to learn it's not all that difficult!

What Services to Offer

One of the big draws of personal assisting to me was the variety of tasks involved. Every day can be different.

Most personal concierges are niched in either the type of clients they service or the type of services they offer.

Grocery shopping

Home organization

Event planning

Buying gifts

Running errands like picking up the kids or dry cleaning

Travel arrangements

Appointment setting

Internet Research

The list goes on and on. And most businesses in this industry offer a specialized yet diverse service list. Stephanie, for example, has a background in interior design. As a result, she told us she can offer "lifestyle consulting and design services in tandem with general concierge services to provide a complete lifestyle resource."

How to Start Your Business

When starting any business, there are a lot of important things to consider:

Do I need to form a business entity such as an LLC or S Corp?

Are there any local business licenses I will need?

Do I need to carry liability and/or indemnity insurance?

These are things you should discuss with your tax preparer, attorney or your local SCORE office. To get things started, prepare a simple business plan. While this isn't always necessary if you won't be applying for financial help, it can help you define your business and target market. B Plans has an example created for a personal concierge business.

Show Me the Money

Depending on the services you offer and your location, you may be able to earn anywhere from $25 to over $100 per hour. Remember, people are paying you for giving them back time. The more time you can free up for them, the more you can charge. Many concierges charge by the month as opposed to billing hourly.

Startup costs are minimal, as are ongoing costs:

Gas

Car Maintenance

Self-employment taxes

Accounting and legal fees

Telephone or cell service

Internet service

Website

Advertising (newspaper or yellow page listing, Facebook ads)

Where to Find Clients

It's important to get out into your community to network and introduce yourself to potential clients. Stephanie started out offering her services to private residences. This not only helped her pay the bills as she built her business, but she was also able to adjust her business model to meet the needs of the clients she wanted to work with in the future. "When working within these residences, I began to observe the needs and wants of my clientele to determine the level of services that would be offered in combination with my previous experience and skill set."

You should also consider local meetups and networking events. These are great places to meet other professionals and possibly joint venture partners.

Rotary clubs

Chamber of Commerce

Meetup.com

There are so many sites these days to help you find clients. Some are free. Some charge a flat fee per listing. Some charge a percentage for every booking they refer you. I highly recommend creating your simple website to attract local clients, but you can also use the following services to meet possibly new prospects.

Instacart – grocery shopping only

Care.com

TaskRabbit

Citizen Shipper – deliveries

Local Facebook Buy/Sell Groups

You can find more on-demand freelance sites in our post, A to Z List of Where to Find Work in the On-Demand Economy.

As with any business, don't overlook your best marketing tool – your clients and friends. A personal referral is cheaper yet more effective than any advertising you can purchase. As Stephanie told us, "referrals are wonderful in the sense that they already provide a level of trust and reliability for any concierge business!"

Understanding the Pros and Cons

This is a great time to be a service provider. Our busy lifestyles have made it acceptable and accessible for the middle class to hire help such as housecleaners, drivers, personal assistants, nannies. These services were once considered a luxury only afforded by the upper class.

That being said, these services are often the first to be cut when times get tight. But don't let that be a detterent! Ride the wave and diversify during the lean times.

Where to Get Help

The concierge industry is still new and evolving. It may not have a lot of training and professional organizations available we see with some industries, but there is help available. Stephanie says, "The ICLM International Concierge and Lifestyle Management is a great resource for concierge companies. The association has a professional database and great professional resources for those starting out.

"It is important to stay aware of the hospitality industry as well as general lifestyle and travel trends."

If you are just getting started, Stephanie has these words of wisdom, "I would advise any concierge beginner never to stop investing in themselves and their service and never to comprise their integrity or core values to get ahead. It's important to maintain a level of optimism and internal motivation when setting corporate goals. Know wholeheartedly that everyone can achieve a level of success. However, the only way that one can do that is by first taking a chance. So take it."

Guide to Starting a Concierge Service Business and Attracting Clients

A concierge service has a broad meaning. Most people associate a concierge as someone at a hotel who helps with booking appointments, arrangements or entertainment plans. However, a concierge can perform many types of tasks for corporate or personal clients. Savvy entrepreneurs have found that saving other people time can be a profitable business. If you are interested in starting a concierge service business, then you will need to take the following steps.

Research Potential Clients

The best way to start a business is to know your customer. If you already know people who could use a concierge service, then try to learn more about similar clients. For example, corporations will hire a concierge to help their employees become more productive. In this case, you should research the types of companies that you wish to service. Once you have a strong understanding of the customer, you will be ready to plan how to meet their needs.

Plan Your Services

After knowing which clients you want to cater to, you are ready to plan which concierge services to offer. To get started, you need to take an inventory of your customer needs. Afterwards, list the strengths and capabilities that you would like your concierge business to have. The business can specialize in FlightHub travel, bookkeeping, running errands, shopping, mailing, managing, etc. Depending on your ideal customers, you can offer a variety of service for a concierge business.

Establish a Concierge Service Location

The concierge service business can run from home or a local office. Start your business by establishing a location. Even if you are getting clients online, a physical location is necessary to get proper business licensing, commercial insurance and documentation. In order to conduct business legally, establish a location. Moreover, people would prefer to work with a quality provider that is local. Especially if you want to work with personal clients, they may want you do carry out tasks in their residential areas.

Start Contacting Potential Clients

With a business started, reach out to clients that would be interested in your service. You can simply start by soliciting to business owners or individuals in your network. To start a concierge service, you just need one client. You can provide them an exceptional level of services and then grow your business through referrals. Or, if you are a more aggressive entrepreneur, you can always directly content many companies and individuals. These are some of the most effective ways to get your first clients. Later on, you can put together a marketing budget and plan to attract more clients.

Invest In Concierge Industry Standards

While the concierge market is young, there are many benchmarks and standards to measure against. You should continue to invest in your hospitality industry knowledge by attending conferences and leadership workshops. As a result, you can train your own team, add services and stay on top of the latest trends. If you continue to improve your concierge service experience, you will attract more clients and grow your new business successfully.

Starting a concierge service business can turn into a successful venture. You have to know your customers, perform tasks efficiently and continue to attract customers. Remember to plan your services when starting out and improve them as you learn more about your customers. Then, focus on providing the best concierge service you can provide in order to earn referrals and attract more clients.

Top Concierge Skills

1. **Communication** - Communication is critical for a concierge. They speak with guests all day, so it is important that they speak clearly and maintain a positive tone and a helpful attitude. Job candidates who are fluent in more than one language will have an advantage when applying for jobs, particularly in major metropolitan areas like New York, Seattle, Los Angeles, Washington DC, and Dallas.

Perhaps most importantly, being a good communicator means being a good listener. Concierges need to listen carefully to their guests' requests to provide a positive experience for them and to proactively identify any particular support they may require.

- Answer Email
- Answer Phone
- Arrange Package Delivery and Pick Up
- Computer
- Confirm Flights and Print Boarding Passes
- Maintain Database of Local Information
- Make and Confirm Reservations
- Marketing
- Microsoft Office
- Order Amenities for Guests' Rooms
- Public Relations
- Secure Tickets for Events
- Sell Tickets to Guests

- Send Pre-Stay Correspondence
- Verbal Communications
- Written Communications

2. **Friendliness** - A concierge is one of the first people a guest sees upon entering a hotel, he or she is the "face" of the organization. Therefore, concierges have to be extremely welcoming. They should greet every guest with a smile and a kind word, no matter how long they've worked or how tired they may be.

- Courtesy Calls to VIP Guests
- Customer Service
- Customer Relations
- Customer Satisfaction
- Greeting Guests

- Guest Relations
- Interpersonal
- Outgoing
- Personable
- Positive Attitude

3. **Organization** - A concierge has to manage multiple tasks at once: they must serve many guests, make appointments and arrangements for people, and more. Being organized allows a concierge to juggle these multiple tasks without losing his or her cool.

- Accommodate Guest Requests
- Airport Transportation

- Coordinate Guest Requests
- Distribute Printed Materials
- Event Planning
- Maintain and Post Daily Event Schedule
- Maintain Menu Books for Local Restaurants

- Maintain Supply of Brochures, Flyers, Handouts, and Maps
- Monitor and Replenish Lobby Refreshments
- Multitasking
- Prioritization
- Provide Business Services
- Schedule Activities
- Set Up Special Packages
- Travel Arrangements

4. **Local Knowledge** - A concierge provides guests with suggestions for entertainment and various services within the hotel itself and in the surrounding geographical area. Therefore, it is very important that a concierge know the area, its best restaurants, and most interesting attractions, and the other sorts of services available in the region.

- Arrange Transportation
- Booking Services
- Booking Show Tickets
- Booking Tours
- Dinner Reservations
- Directions

- Knowledge of Hotel / Resort Features
- Knowledge of Local Dining, Entertainment, Theater, Shows, and Events
- Recommendations
- Strong Knowledge of Local Area

5. **Professionalism** - Because a concierge is representing the hotel and is interacting directly with guests, he or she must look and act professionally. Professional attire and demeanor will make guests trust the concierge and his or her suggestions.

- Conflict Resolution

- Dependability
- Flexibility
- Patience
- Professionally Promote Resort Activities to Guests
- Punctuality
- Telephone Etiquette

By demonstrating your professionalism, communication skills, local knowledge, organizational talents, and friendliness on your resume and in your interview, you're sure to impress the hiring manager as being a great choice for their next concierge.

How to Start a Personal Concierge Business

Some of the links included in this article are from our advertisers. Read our Advertiser Disclosure.

Person working at their computer mixing sound with a microphone nearby and speakers

Do you want to make money by running errands and taking care of those minute daily tasks that busy professionals and the affluent don't have time to complete? If so, you might consider starting your own personal concierge business.

With minimal startup costs and the ability to perform a variety of tasks, this can be the perfect business opportunity you're looking to work from home.

What Is a Personal Concierge Business?

A personal concierge service is a very open-ended job description as you will most likely perform a variety of tasks. Maybe the best way of describing a personal concierge is the in-person version of a virtual assistant.

Your client can range from the rich and affluent, businesses, to regular working professionals. No matter who your client is, you can expect to perform a combination of the following tasks:

- Appointment setting
- Basic repairs
- Buying groceries
- Cooking meals
- Dog walking
- Dropping off dry cleaning
- Internet research
- Light home or office cleaning
- Mailing packages
- Organizing weekly schedule
- Picking up children from school

- Planning events and parties
- Waiting for repair technicians to arrive during the workday

Each client has different concierge needs so you might perform many of the tasks listed above and a few that aren't listed here.

Because you have the opportunity to perform a variety of tasks with a flexible schedule, you can be an ideal candidate if you enjoy being a "jack of all trades."

For example, you might tire of exclusively being a Lyft driver or answering emails for other clients. For some, variety truly is the spice of life and becoming a personal concierge can be the calling you're looking for.

How Much Money Can You Make as a Personal Concierge?

As a personal concierge, you can expect to charge between $25 and $150 per hour. This income stream can also replace your current day job as you can potentially earn between $40,000 and $60,000 annually. How much you make mostly depends on the services you perform and how many hours you want to work each week.

As with any new business venture, it might take some time to build a steady client base so you might have to first start your concierge business as a side hustle in your free time. As you add clients or offer additional services, you can scale your business to maybe even hire assistants if you choose.

Charge Annual Membership Fees

You might also consider charging your clients an annual or monthly membership fee. This is a common practice for personal concierge businesses and other "assistant" positions as you earn a predictable salary, even when clients don't need your services as frequently.

To get an idea, you might consider comparing the membership fee rates that other local concierge services charge for similar services.

How Much does it Cost to Become a Personal Concierge?

One reason why you might consider becoming a personal concierge is the minimal startup costs involved. You don't have to rent office space or borrow money to purchase expensive equipment. It's entirely possible to launch your business from your kitchen table and use the tools and skills you already possess.

Some of the items you will need include:

- Phone (Potentially a landline with an answering machine or an 800 number)
- Computer with Internet access
- A website that lists your available services and contact information
- Accounting software like Intuit Quickbooks
- Reliable vehicle
- Any supplies needed for cleaning, basic repairs, or other services you offer

Insurance

There's a good chance you already own everything you need to land your first client, so now you can proceed with building your client base and getting paid.

Make a Business Plan

With every new business, you need to have a business plan to determine how much you need to make to profit from your efforts. Nobody wants to work for free, so you need to accurately calculate your bottom dollar so your personal concierge business can succeed.

Because you won't be applying for a business loan like a brick-and-mortar business, your business plan only needs to be one page because you might only share it with your business coach or friends you ask for advice.

Set an Advertising Budget

Maybe you already have a client list you can pull from to offer concierge services too. If so, count your blessings. But if you're truly starting your business from the ground up, you will probably need to do some advertising.

Word of mouth advertising is almost always the best advertising source, so your first step should be asking your family and friends if they know of anybody that can benefit from your services. Plus, this advertising method is completely free which is a huge benefit for a fledgling entrepreneur.

After that, you need to consider advertising on Facebook, your local online classifieds like Craigslist, and even posting business cards and flyers at local businesses or public places including your local library, community center, or gym. Because paid advertising can become expensive quickly, spend a few dollars in digital and print advertising to see which method has the best response.

Join Your Local Chamber of Commerce

You might also consider joining your local Chamber of Commerce to network with local business leaders and establish a community presence. Networking is a very important part in many facets of life.

Sometimes, it only takes rubbing shoulders with a business leader, church members, or fellow civic organization members to make a connection that eventually leads to a future client.

By being able to connect a face with your name, you can establish credibility. Since you are responsible for completing your client's personal or business errands, potential clients may want to meet you before they trust you with their personal information.

How to Get Your First Client

Having a local and online presence is crucial to attracting concierge clients. In addition to any physical and social media advertising you do, you should also consider creating a profile on some of the following concierge websites:

- Care
- Instacart
- TaskRabbit

On these websites, you can advertise your complete suite of services to for one-time and recurring clients. Listing your name on as many platforms as possible increases the probability of attracting your first client.

As you receive good feedback, your reputation and personal brand will grow so it's easier to attract future clients with less effort. This is because your caliber of service speaks for itself and your reputation reflects positively.

As your confidence level grows, you can begin increasing your rates and you will also know where to look for new clients. Hopefully, your previous clients will refer you to their friends so you can spend more time making money instead of searching for clients.

Offer Free or Discounted Services

You still want to price your services competitively so you don't look like a swindler or incapable of doing a good job, but you might have to charge lower rates initially to attract your first clients. One potential way to attract clients is to offer free services if the client agrees to pay for several other services.

This free service can be performed weekly, monthly, semi-annually. If you're computer savvy, you might offer to back up their data to a cloud network periodically or ensure the latest software updates have been installed. We all have a unique gift, so find your "unfair advantage" that sets you apart from everybody else.

Additional Tips to Make More Money as a Personal Concierge

Starting your own personal concierge business is an exciting time. Your first few months might be the most difficult as you charge lower rates to establish long-term clients.

Making as much money possible can be more important as a new business with low cash flow. Having less money in your bank account each month means you have a smaller financial cushion to grow your business and saving for future expenses.

These tips can help you boost your profit margins in the short-term so you can focus on building your business.

Shop With Cash Back Apps

Knowing how much to charge is one part of the equation to operating a successful business. The second half of the equation is keeping your business expenses to a minimum.

Two obvious ways are driving the most fuel-efficient car possible and using the resources you already have available instead of buying a completely new inventory for each client. If you're client provides the supplies, that's a different story.

The easiest way to reduce costs is to use these apps when you shop for your clients:

- Rakuten
- Ibotta
- Swagbucks

These three apps help you earn cash rewards when you shop online. The Ibotta app is perfect for buying groceries as you earn bonus cash on many grocery items by activating the offers and scanning a copy of your receipt.

Follow-Up With Previous Customers

Follow-up is also a key ingredient to success because you already have an existing relationship with your clients. You're running personal errands for busy people that might forget to call you for future work. Communication is a two-way street, so don't be afraid to give them a call or send a text message asking if they need any help.

It only takes a few minutes to make a call or send a brief message. Since you might not work for that client currently, the only thing you have to lose is a few minutes of time if they don't need your services again.

Another important reason to follow-up is to ask for feedback. These conversations can be an excellent way to discover how you excel and where you can improve. If feedback isn't important, why do you think so many customers offer paid surveys to get consumer opinions and conduct market research?

Learn New Skills

When you're not running errands or pitching new clients, take the time to learn new skills. As you talk with potential clients, you will find out what concierge services busy professionals in your town need. If you aren't the most Confident In Some Of These Areas, Practice Them At Home Or Take A Video Class On Skillshare.

The Concept Of Learning Something New Every Day Doesn't Have To End When You Finish School!

Steps to Naming your Concierge Business

This four-step process will help you name your concierge business. In this example, I created names that exemplify luxury and comfort. Here's each step I took in crafting these business names.

1) Brainstorm your name ideas

Brainstorming on the words you want to use to represent your business is very important because this is the first impression your business makes on your potential customers. I decided to use words like help, errands, and assistant to illustrate stress relief and constant help. Your goal here is to create a list of words or names that come to mind when thinking about your business.

If you're stuck on words to use, try our business name generator.

Here are my name ideas after brainstorming:

ProConcierge Life Saver The Time Fairy Concier de Girl Rent an Assistant Trip Aid U-Booker WebConcierge Team Concierge The Concierge Co. ProCon Dr. Do Help Hub Front Desk Fairy Full Spectrum Concierge On The Goers Task

Rabbit Easy Errands Life Planner Co. Plan It

2) **Shortlist your ideas**

Once you've developed a list of possible names, do an analysis of your ideas. Remove any names that could be hard to remember, spell or speak aloud. Keep names that are brandable, sound great, are memorable and communicate your brand values, product or service to your target audience.

Here's a quick checklist you can run your ideas through to help shorten your list of name:

- Is the name simple and easy to remember?
- Is the name easy to read and say aloud?
- Is the name different from competitors?
- Does the name convey a relevant meaning?
- Does the name avoid overused words or cliches?

My Shortlist:

The Time Fairy Concier de Girl Trip Aid Rent an Assistant

Removed Ideas:

ProConcierge Life Saver U-Booker WebConcierge Team Concierge The Concierge Co. ProCon Dr. Do Help Hub Front Desk Fairy Full Spectrum Concierge On The Goers Task Rabbit Easy Errands Life Planner Co. Plan It

Create a unique business name with a Business name Generator

Enter words and click generate...

Check domain availability with GoDaddy

Generate

3) **Get some feedback**

You'll now have a list of 3-6 great concierge business names and you can start to ask potential customers or people working in the industry for feedback (your target audience). Avoid feedback from family and friends, are more likely to praise all your ideas and they aren't your customer.

Be sure to ask questions like:

- What first comes to mind when you first hear the name?
- How would you spell it?
- With your customer feedback you can now ask yourself is the name still relevant? and did it represent your business how you intended?

My customer feedback:

Trip Aid

This sounds like a traveling assistant.

Rent an Assistant

This sounds like a company that provides assistance for hire.

Concier de Girl

This sounds like a very catchy concierge name.

The Time Fairy

This sounds like a time maximization effect.

4) **Check if it's available**

At this point, it's good to have at least three great concierge business names on your list, in case your any of your names are already taken. You can do a quick Business Name Search online to find out if your name is available within your country/state, also be sure to search if the name is also available for Trademark and Domain name Registration.

Check Domain Availability

check domain availability

Check

Competitor Name Analysis

To help you brainstorm potential business names, let's take a look at three successful concierge businesses and break down why and how they've chosen to name their business and why it works for them.

Quintessentially Logo

Quintessentially is a very catchy name and has managed to combine the queen and essential to illustrate both luxurious and basic needs.

The Billionaire Concierge Logo

The Billionaire Concierge is a name that illustrates luxury and comfort at it's highest level. It denotes a high standard and service.

Knightsbridge Circle Logo

Knightsbridge Circle is a name that illustrates effectiveness and high performance. It also creates a link between those two qualities and the provision of service by the use of the word Bridge.

More Tips for naming your concierge business

The ideal business name should be simple, memorable and convey a meaning all at the same time. Here are my tips to keep in mind when developing your business names.

1. Do a Competitor Analysis

Doing a competitor analysis as your first step will save you a lot of time in the future, knowing what names to avoid and understanding why and how your competitors business name words for them will help you in forming your own business names. When analyzing competitors think about:

- What business or product values are they conveying in their

business name? How does that work for them?
- Is there a trend in how these businesses are naming themselves? It's best to avoid sounding like "just another one of those businesses".
- Who does it best? Why does it work and how can I produce a better name?

2. Focus on Naming your Business not Describing it.

Avoid describing your business literally, as this will lead to the use of overused words like help, maid or luggage. A more effective business name should convey to customers your businesses and product values at a deeper level. Try name your business in a way that has a story behind it.

Let's take for example a real concierge business named "Quintessentially".

Literally, this name is both qualitative and classy.

3. How to make a more memorable name

Creating a memorable business name is the first step in getting into a customers mind and is also a task that's easier said than done. Your business name should aim to stop a customer in their tracks and give an extra thought on your product among your wave of competitors. Some tips to create a memorable name would be:

Use rhythmic pronunciation or alliteration (Easy Errands, Help Hub)

Try using a word that wouldn't be relevant when out of context (Task Rabbit: Rabbits are extremely fast and devoted animals, and in this context, it is used to mean a very fast task operator)

Keep it short and simple.

4. Try purchasing a Brandable business name

Brandable business names are names that are non-sensical but read and are pronounced well. They often use letter patterns of Vowel/Consonant/Vowel as these word structures are typically short, catchy and easy to say and remember. For example, some brandable concierge business names could be:

Concier de Girl

U-Booker

Conduit Kings

You can find a full list of Brandable business names at Domainify.com

5. Avoid combining words just to create a unique name.

Another mistake business owners typically make is creating bad word combinations when they find out that their business name idea is already taken. For example, shortening Conduit King to ConK or Con King.

You can see how these ideas are a step backward as they are not catchy, easily pronounceable or memorable. In these situations, we suggest starting from scratch and trying the tips we mentioned previously.

Business Name Ideas

Here's the ultimate list of related words you could use in your business name. Below is a list of trending, descriptive and action words that are often related to.

www.ingramcontent.com/pod-product-compliance
Lightning Source LLC
Chambersburg PA
CBHW070147230526
45471CB00002B/561